Praying with
Mother Teresa

EDITED BY ROSWITHA KORNPROBST

TRANSLATED BY THE
SCHOOL SISTERS OF NOTRE DAME

PAULIST PRESS
New York/Mahwah, NJ

Cover photo by Hiroshi Katayanagi, SJ
Cover design by Sharyn Banks
Book design by Lynn Else

Title of the original German edition: *Roswitha Kornprobst, Beten Mit Mutter Teresa*. Copyright © Butzon & Bercker GmbH, Kevelaer, Germany, www.bube.de

English translation copyright © 2011 by Paulist Press, Inc.

All rights reserved. No part of this book may be reproduced or transmitted in any form or by any means, electronic or mechanical, including photocopying, recording, or by any information storage and retrieval system without permission in writing from the Publisher.

Library of Congress Cataloging-in-Publication Data

Beten Mit Mutter Teresa. English.
   Praying with Mother Teresa / edited by Roswitha Kornprobst ; translated by the School Sisters of Notre Dame.
     p. cm.
   ISBN 978-0-8091-4526-3 (alk. paper)
   1. Catholic Church—Prayers and devotions. 2. Prayer—Catholic Church. 3. Teresa, Mother, 1910–1997. I. Kornprobst, Roswitha, 1957– II. Title.
   BX2149.2.B48 2011
   242′.802—dc22

2010035328

Published by Paulist Press
997 Macarthur Boulevard
Mahwah, New Jersey 07430

www.paulistpress.com

Printed and bound in the
United States of America

Contents

Introduction: Mother Teresa: A Person of Prayer v
1. Make Us Worthy, Lord: *Prayers for Every Day* 1
2. Lead Me According to Your Will:
   Prayers to Follow Christ 6
3. Father, Help Me to Know You: *Prayers to God* 10
4. Lord, Help Us: *Prayers to Jesus* 14
5. To Be a Light for Others: *Prayers for Peace and Unity* 18
6. Take, Lord, Whatever I Have: *Prayers of Coworkers
   of Mother Teresa* 25
7. Mother of Jesus, Give Me Your Heart:
   Prayers to Mary 29
8. Lord, I Need You Now: *Short Prayers* 31
9. Take Up Your Cross and Follow Me: *Mother Teresa's
   Way of the Cross* 35
10. Branches on Jesus the Vine: *Contemplative Thoughts* 39
About the Editor 47

Introduction

MOTHER TERESA: A PERSON OF PRAYER

Mother Teresa passed away on September 5, 1997. The diminutive, wrinkled woman in the white sari with blue borders, who stood out among others and who was admired by the whole world, is now resting in heaven, as she so desired. The recipient of a Nobel Peace Prize in 1979, she was a thorn in our conscience. As "one of the most important personalities of our time" (according to Pope John Paul II), she provided a measuring rod for resolving the issues that confront our common humanity. On October 19, 2003, she was beatified in Rome as a holy woman of the twentieth century. In his sermon during the beatification Mass, Pope John Paul II said:

> Deeply touched, we today remember Mother Teresa as an outstanding servant of the poor, of the church, and of the entire world. Her life is a witness to the dignity and superiority of humble service. She did not only want to

be the last, but to be the servant of the last. Like a true mother of the poor, she bent down to all who suffered from the various forms of poverty. Her greatness consisted in her ability to give without counting the cost, to give "until it hurts!" Her life was one of radical existence, a courageous proclamation of the Gospel.

The sisters of the religious community that Mother Teresa founded in 1950, the Missionaries of Charity, live strictly according to the Gospel. To enable them to lead this difficult life with the poorest of the poor, their daily routine is closely connected with the Holy Eucharist and prayer. The Mass is their spiritual nourishment. The sisters receive their power from God through prayer. One of the sisters expressed it this way: "Without prayer, I could not work the way I do, even for a half hour." Another sister said, "Each morning I awaken with the knowledge that the day will again have difficulties, but prayer gives us strength, helps us, and gives us joy in what we are doing and have to do. We begin the day with prayer and Holy Mass, and we end the day with an hour of adoration." Mother Theresa emphasized: "Without HIM, we can do nothing. It is at the altar where we meet the suffering poor. In HIM, we see that suffering is the way to greater love and generosity."

In the Eucharist the sisters see Christ in the form of bread; in the slums they touch Christ in wasted bodies and neglected children. For the sisters, the Holy Eucharist and the poor are one love. To be able to fulfill their work, they need a deep union with Christ through meditative prayer. The strength, joy, and love of these Missionaries of Charity are founded on their connection with the Holy Eucharist through their prayer.

Prayer Makes the Heart Spacious

Throughout her life Mother Teresa emphasized again and again the importance of prayer: "It is impossible to work in this apostolate without being a woman of prayer, without forgetting oneself, and without the determination to fulfill the will of God. We must recognize our union with Christ as he recognized his union with his Father. Our actions will become apostolic only if we permit him to work through us with his power, his desire, and his love." She often encouraged her sisters: "Love to pray—you should often feel it necessary to pray during the day—and make an effort to pray. Prayer enlarges the heart until it is able to hold God, who has given himself to you. Pray and search, and your heart will become large enough to receive him and keep him as your own.

God Is the Friend of Silence

Mother Teresa always began her prayer with a period of silence because God speaks to us in the stillness of our hearts:

Prayer is very difficult if one does not know how to pray. Therefore we have to help each other learn it. The most important element is stillness. We cannot place ourselves into the presence of God if we do not bring ourselves to an inner and exterior quiet. We must become accustomed to a stillness of the Spirit in the eyes and on the tongue. God is a friend of stillness. We must find God, but we will not find him in noise or activity.

The more we receive during our quiet prayer, the more we can give in our active life. Silence gives us new insight for everything. We need silence to be able to touch hearts. What we have to say is not important, but what God tells us and wants to say through us is essential.

A Little Exultation of the Heart

Mother Teresa's attitudes toward prayer are timeless:

Prayer nourishes the soul—what blood is for the body, prayer is for the soul—and it brings us nearer to God. If you are searching for God and do not know how to start, learn to pray.

One can pray any time, anywhere. Simply talk to God. Tell him everything. Talk with him. He is our Father. We are all created by God; we are his children. If we pray we will receive the answer we need. You should spend in prayer at least one half hour in the morning and an hour in the evening. You can pray while you are working. Work does not stop your prayer. You need only to lift your heart to him and say: "I love you, God. I trust in you. I believe in you. I need you now." Little prayers like that are wonderful prayers.

These are small movements of the heart that are very helpful. In that way prayer, even if it is short, becomes a power to support our life:

> Begin and end your day with prayer. When you pray, thank God for all his gifts. When you trust in God, you can overcome all your feelings of doubt through the power of prayer.

The Power of Prayer

Again and again Mother Teresa asked for prayer for herself and for her sisters and brothers. The Missionaries of Charity trust in God and proceed—praying—through every distress. In their life and in their work they have become aware of the power of prayer and the deep trust in God who fulfills their prayer: "Pray for us that our work for God is not useless, because it is his work."

A priest tells about one of the many examples of the power of prayer and God's loving answer to the sisters in Calcutta:

> I was on the way to see the work of Mother Teresa and the Missionaries of Charity and decided to stop at their motherhouse to attend Holy Mass there. At the entrance I was greeted by one of the sisters who said, "Thank God that you are here, Father. Please come in." Since I was not wearing my clerical garb, I responded, "How do you know that I am a priest?" She answered, "The priest who

usually celebrates Mass here could not come today so we prayed to God to send us another priest."

Mother Teresa's presence was a living prayer. For her it was as necessary to withdraw from the crowd to be alone with God as it was necessary for her to work. She considered prayer her all-important work. For her the gift of prayer was a present from God. "Often a single glimpse of Christ is the best prayer: I look at him and he looks at me. That is the most perfect prayer."

Chapter One
MAKE US WORTHY, LORD

PRAYERS FOR EVERY DAY

Daily prayer for the Missionaries of Charity and the coworkers of Mother Teresa:

> Make us worthy, Lord,
> to serve our neighbors
> in the entire world,
> especially those who live and die
> in poverty and hunger.
>
> Give them
> through our hands
> their daily bread,
> and peace and joy
> through our understanding love.

Lord,
make me an instrument of your peace.
Where there is hatred, let me bring love;
where injustice rules, the spirit of forgiveness;
where there is disunity, give us unity;
where there is confusion, give us truth;
where doubt, confidence;
where despair, hope;
where shadow, light;
and where sadness, joy.

Lord, let me seek not to be consoled, but to console,
not to be understood, but to understand,
not to be loved, but to love.
Then those who give of themselves will receive;
who forget themselves, will find themselves;
who forgive, will receive forgiveness;
and who die, will be awakened
to eternal life.
Amen.

The second and third stanzas of this prayer are credited to St. Francis of Assisi. Sometimes Mother Teresa added a prayer of her own:

Lord,
let each sister see Christ
in the person of the poor.
The more repelling the work
or the person is,

the greater must be
the faith, the love,
and the joyful dedication
when she serves you, our Lord,
in pitiful disguise.

The well-known prayer in a different translation:

Lord, make me a channel of your peace.
Where there is hatred, let me bring love.
Where there is injustice,
let me bring the spirit of forgiveness.
Where there is discord, let me bring harmony.
Where error, let me bring truth.
Where doubt, let me bring faith.
Where there is despair, let me bring hope.
Where there is darkness, light,
and where there is sadness, joy.

Lord,
Let me try to console, rather than be consoled.
To understand, than be understood.
To love, than be loved.
Because when one forgets himself, he will be found.
When one forgives, he will be forgiven.
And when one dies,
He will awake to eternal life.

Daily prayer during work with the sick:

> Suffering Christ, help me
> to see you today and every day
> in the person of the sick,
> that I serve you
> by taking care of them.
> Let me see you even under the repulsive masks of
> anger, crime, or irrationality
> so I can say
> "My suffering Jesus, how good it is to serve you."
>
> Lord, show me that faith,
> then my work will never be monotonous.
> I will find joy if I accept moods
> and fulfill the wishes of these poor sufferers.
>
> Dear sick person,
> I love you so much more
> because you are a likeness of Christ;
> I consider it an honor
> to be able to work with you.
>
> O God,
> since you are the suffering Jesus,
> in your goodness, be also for me
> a patient Jesus
> who overlooks my mistakes
> and only recognizes
> that I wish to love you

and want to serve you
in each of your suffering children.

Lord, increase my faith.
Bless my efforts and my work
now and forever.
Amen.

I pray
and through my prayer
I become one
with the love of Christ.
I realize
that prayer means
to live in him,
to love him, which again means
to make his words come true.

For me to pray means
to be one with the will of Jesus
for twenty-four hours each day,
to live
for him,
through him,
and with him.

Chapter Two

LEAD ME ACCORDING TO YOUR WILL

PRAYERS TO FOLLOW CHRIST

Don't look for God in faraway countries. He is not there. He is very near to you. Let the light burn and you will always see him. Keep lighting your lamp and you will always see his love and recognize how good is the God whom you love.

Lord,
open our eyes so we can recognize you in
our brothers and sisters.

Lord,
open our ears so we can hear the call of the hungry
and those suffering from the cold,
of those who are afraid
and those who are oppressed.

Lord,
open our hearts that we can love others
the way you love us.

Renew in us your spirit, Lord.
Make us free and united.

Lord,
grant that I may recognize
the dignity of my vocation with all its responsibilities.
Do not let me lose it through
hardness, wickedness, or impatience.

Lord,
you are the only one.
Everything is for you.
Use me, lead me, according to your will.
Father, not as I will,
but as you will it.

With free choice, my God,
and out of love for you,
I will remain and do
whatever your holy will
may command me to do.
At this moment
give me courage.

My God, I am yours.
I trust in your word
and your calling.
You are not going to let me fall.
Amen.

The following prayer is said by all Missionary Brothers and Sisters of Charity before they begin their apostolate:

Dear God, Great Healer,
I kneel before you
because each perfect gift must come from you.
I pray you, give my hands dexterity,
my mind sharp understanding,
my heart compassion and tenderness.
Give me purposeful behavior and the power
to take upon myself the burden
of my suffering companions
and the true realization of the honor
which has been given to me.
Take from my heart all falsehood
and all worldly desire so I can
trust in you with the simple faith
of a child.

Once you learn the art
of consideration for others

you will become
ever more like Christ.

All our words
would be useless
if they did not come
from inside us.
Words that do not reflect
the light of Christ
increase the darkness.

We all must follow Christ
to the place of crucifixion
if we want to be resurrected
with him.

Before his death Christ gave us
his Body and his Blood
so we have life and courage within us
to carry the cross
and follow him step by step.

Chapter Three

FATHER, HELP ME TO KNOW YOU

PRAYERS TO GOD

Father, glorify your Son
so that your Son may glorify you.
Help us to glorify him through us, your unworthy
    servants,
because we came here
for his glory, for his exultation.
For that reason we work, suffer, and pray.
What we do, we do for Jesus.
Our life does not make sense
if we are not here for him alone.
May all people get to know him
and so reach eternal life, which he has purchased
    for us.
Father, this is eternal life:
to know you, the only true God.

and him whom you have sent,
Jesus Christ.
Let us take this message
of eternal life to the poor!
May they who otherwise
must live without any consolation
or any possession find you,
love you, and have part of you
and life eternal.
Then you are God and
Father of all people
with our Lord Jesus Christ,
source and fountain of all truth,
all goodness and happiness.
Let us lead to you all whom we meet,
those who work with us and for us,
those we assist in their hour of death,
those who come to us
like the children came to Jesus
whom he blessed,
like the sick whom he healed,
like the suffering whom he consoled.

O God,
We believe that you are here.
We adore you, we love you,
with our whole heart and soul
because you are worthy of our love
to the highest degree.
We long for you, we love you, as much
as the blessed in heaven love you.
We honor all plans of your Divine Providence
and give ourselves completely
to your will.
We love our neighbor as ourselves
because of you.
We honestly forgive all
who have hurt us
and beg pardon of those
whom we have offended.

How wonderful it is to know
that God loves us.
I hope that as many people as possible
get to know God, to love him,
and to serve him
because that is true happiness.

To be happy with God means
you love as he loves;
you help as he helps;

you give as he gives;
you serve as he serves;
you heal as he heals.

God does not stop loving the world.
He sends us into the world
to be his love and his mercy.

Chapter Four
LORD, HELP US

PRAYERS TO JESUS

Lord, help us
that we may learn to bear
the difficulties and pains of daily life,
and are able to be strengthened
by your death on the cross
and your resurrection,
so we can grow into an
evermore creative fullness of life.
You have accepted the depths
of human life,
and the pain of your suffering
and your crucifixion,
patiently and humbly.
Help us that we may accept
the troubles and difficulties
that each new day brings
as a welcome opportunity

to grow as a human person
and to become more like you.
Make us able to receive them patiently
and increase in ourselves trust in your assistance.
Let us recognize the fact
that we can reach a full life only
if we constantly die to ourselves
and to our egoistic desires,
because only through dying with you
can we rise with you.
Amen.

Redeem me, O Jesus,
from the desire to be loved,
from the desire to be famous,
from the desire to be honored,
from the desire to be praised,
from the desire to be preferred,
from the desire to be asked for advice,
from the desire to be recognized,
from the fear of being humiliated,
from the fear of being scorned,
from the fear of being scolded,
from the fear of being slandered,
from the fear of being forgotten,
from the fear of being treated unfairly,
from the fear of being mocked,
from the fear of being suspected of evil.

What is Jesus for me?
The Word made flesh,
the Bread of Life,
the Sacrificial Lamb who died on the cross
for our sins,
the Sacrifice offered during Holy Mass
for the sins of the world
and for my sins…

The Word that must be said,
the Truth that must be announced,
the Way that must be taken,
the Light that must be enkindled,
the Life that must be lived,
the Love that must be loved,
the Joy that must be shared,
the Peace that must be passed on…

The hungry who must be fed,
the lonely who must be loved,
the unwelcome who must be accepted…

For me, Jesus is my God.
Jesus is my bridegroom.
Jesus is my life.
Jesus is my only love.
Jesus is my all in all.

Chapter Five

TO BE A LIGHT FOR OTHERS

PRAYERS FOR PEACE AND UNITY

The following prayer of John Henry Newman was greatly loved by Mother Teresa because it expressed her own spirituality. She often sent it to coworkers and helpers, and gave it to visitors for guidance and help in their service to their neighbor:

> Dear Lord, help me
> to spread your fragrance
> wherever I go.
>
> Flood my soul with your spirit and life,
> penetrate my whole being,
> and take me as your complete possession
> so that my whole life
> radiates only you.
>
> Shine through me
> and live in me in such a way

that all who come in contact with me
feel your presence in me.
Let them look up
and no longer see me
but only you, O Jesus.

Stay with me.
Then I will begin to shine
as you are shining,
to shine so that I become a light for others.
The light, O Jesus, will come from you.
None of it is mine.
It is you
who will shine for others through me.

Let me praise you in the way
that you love most,
if I become a light
for the people around me.
Let me announce you
without speaking, without words,
through my example,
through the captivating power
of what I am doing,
the sincere fullness of love
which my heart holds for you.
   —*Cardinal John Henry Newman (original English version)*

Another prayer that Mother Teresa loved and often gave away is the following prayer of Cardinal Montini, Pope Paul VI:

> Lord, make us worthy
> to serve our companion human beings
> throughout the world.
> To those who live and die in poverty and hunger,
> give them today, through our hands,
> their daily bread,
> and give them peace and joy
> through our understanding love.
>
> —*Pope Paul VI*

> Where there is peace, there is God.
> Works of love will always be works of peace.
>
> —*Mother Teresa*

Therefore, we petition God, that he will fill our hearts with love and peace:

> Lead us from death to life,
> from falsehood to truth.
> Lead us from despair to hope,
> from fear to truth.

> Lead us from hatred to love,
> from war to peace.

Let peace fill our hearts,
our world, our universe.
Peace! Peace! Peace!

Mother Teresa and Roger Schutz, the founder of the Taizé ecumenical monastic community, were deeply disturbed by the suffering in the world today. They could not rest when they saw the wounds of humanity. The divisions among Christians are unbearable. Are we going to give up our differences and free ourselves of the fear of one another? Why do we always look to see who is right or wrong? In our search for reconciliation will we ever learn to give our best and to accept the best of others with the same love for one another with which Christ loves us?

Jesus Christ,
we thank you for making the Catholic Church
the Church of the Eucharist,
rooted in your words
"This is my Body,
This is my Blood,"
that it may give life
through your miraculous presence.

We thank you also for the Evangelical Churches,
which are Churches of the Word
who constantly call to mind
the power of the Gospel.

We thank you
that the Orthodox Churches
in their faithfulness
throughout history
were led to the uttermost
boundaries of love.

Your Church
becomes the leaven
for the community of the poor
on earth and for
the entire family of mankind.
Amen.

Christ, open us all
to grow beyond ourselves
and no longer delay to be reconciled
to this unique community
that carries the name "Church,"
irreplaceable leaven in the
pulp of humanity.
Amen.

On August 16, 1976, Mother Teresa and Prior Roger Schutz composed the following prayer on the occasion of the Youth Council in Taizé:

O God, Father of all people,
you call us all
to carry love where the poor are downtrodden,
joy where the Church is discouraged,
reconciliation where people are separated—
father from son,
mother from daughter,
husband from wife,
those who believe from those who don't believe,
the Christian from his unloved Christian brother.
You prepare our way
so that the wounded Body of Christ,
your Church,
may become the leaven
for the community of the poor on earth and
for the entire family of mankind.
Amen.

Be a living expression
of God's goodness
through goodness in your face,
goodness in your eyes,
goodness in your smile,
goodness in your warm greeting.

All our words will be for nothing
unless they come from the depth
of our hearts.

Smiles create smiles
just as love creates love.

Smile at everyone.
That will help you
to live with one another
with greater love.

Always be happy.
Give all who suffer
or are lonely
a happy smile.

Chapter Six

TAKE, LORD, WHATEVER I HAVE

PRAYERS OF COWORKERS OF MOTHER TERESA

Lord, take from me
all my indifference,
all my apathy
toward the needs of the poor.
When I meet you in the hungry,
the thirsty, the strangers,
show me how to quench
your hunger and your thirst.
Show me how I can receive you
in my house and in my heart.

Take, Lord, and receive
all my liberty
and my memory,
my understanding

and my will.
All that I have and own
I have received from you.

To you, Lord, I return what is yours.
Do with it whatever you want.
Only give me your love and your grace.
That is enough for me.

Lord, let us be faithful to each other
in your love.
Do not allow anything or anyone
to separate us from your love
or the love we should have
for one another.
Amen.

Do you need my hands, Lord,
to help the sick and the poor
who need help today?
Lord, I give you my hands today.

Do you need my feet, Lord,
to carry me today to those
who need a friend?
Lord, I give you my feet today.

Do you need my voice, Lord,
that I may speak the work of love
to those who need it today?
Lord, I give you my voice.

Do you need my heart, Lord,
so that I may love each person today
without exception?
Lord, I give you my heart today.

Lord, give me an open heart
that I may recognize you.
Give me an idea of heaven in the bud,
an experience of heaven
in the smallest deed of charity.

>Everything we do is done for Jesus.
>We live for Jesus.
>Jesus came to this world
>to bring us the good news,
>to tell us that he loves us
>and that he wants us
>to love each other
>as he has loved us.
>Let us love one another
>as he loved us on the cross
>and loves us in the Eucharist.

There is no greater love
than the love of Jesus.
There is no greater joy
than the joy of Jesus.
Let the light of Christ
always burn in our hearts,
because he alone is the way we can walk,
the life we can live,
the love that gives us the
strength to love.
With Jesus everything is possible
because God is love.

Chapter Seven

MOTHER OF JESUS, GIVE ME YOUR HEART

PRAYERS TO MARY

Mary, the humble maiden of the Lord and Mother of God, was for Mother Teresa and is for her sisters an example of faith. The way leads them to Christ, to his loving heart, through Mary, the best of all mothers. Following is one of the prayers the sisters pray frequently:

> Mary, Mother of Jesus,
> give me your heart,
> so beautiful, so pure, so unspotted,
> so full of love and humility,
> so that I will be able
> to receive Jesus, the Bread of Life;
> to love him as you have loved him
> and to serve him
> in the shocking appearance
> of the poorest of the poor.

Prayer is joy.
Prayer is the sunshine of the love of God.
Prayer is hoping for eternal happiness.
Prayer is the burning flame of God's love
to and for me.
Let us ask our Dear Lady to give us her heart,
so beautiful, so pure, so spotless,
so full of love and humility,
that we may be able to pray as she prayed,
to love Jesus as she loved Jesus,
to stand as totally before her Father as she did,
to be the faithful bride of the Holy Spirit
as she was.
Let us pray for one another
because this is the best way to love one another
as Jesus told us:
Love one another as he has loved us.

Mary is our mother from morning to evening.
We have a mother in heaven, Mary, the source of our joy.
Pray to her; pray the Rosary.
She will guide us to Christ.

Chapter Eight
LORD, I NEED YOU NOW
SHORT PRAYERS

I love you, God.
I trust in you.
I believe in you.
I need you now.

Lord,
let me become holy
according to your own heart,
humble and gentle.

My God, my God,
what is a heart
that you desire it
and overwhelm it

with your heart
as if there were nothing else for you!
Amen.

We offer you all the thoughts of our spirit,
the feelings of our heart.
Let us hear your voice
and follow your inspirations.
Amen.

Mary,
Mother of God,
be a mother to me now.
Help me to pray.

Come, Holy Spirit,
lead me, protect me.
Clear my spirit
so I can pray.

Lord, I am sorry
that I hurt you.
I will try
not to offend you again.

My God, I love you.
My God, I am sorry.
My God, I believe in you.
My God, I trust in you.
Help us to love one another
as you love us.

Jesus, you are in my heart.
I believe in your tender love for me.
I love you.

Jesus, you are my God.
Jesus, you are my life.
Jesus, you are my only love.
Jesus, you are my one and all.

It is God's greatest gift for you
to have the strength
to accept with a smile
whatever he gives you.

We must have a smile
for each child we help,
for each neglected person

with whom we keep company,
for every sick person
to whom we distribute medicine.

Whenever you give away a smile,
it is an act of love,
a present for that person,
something wonderful.

Always have a smile ready.
Have time for your neighbor.

Chapter Nine

TAKE UP YOUR CROSS AND FOLLOW ME

MOTHER TERESA'S WAY OF THE CROSS

Composed for the youth of the world for the International Eucharistic Congress, August 16, 1976.

Jesus said to the youth of his time: "Whoever wants to be my disciple, take up your cross and follow me."

Before he carried his own cross, he knew we needed him to be able to follow him—and that we cannot carry our cross alone.

So he changed himself into the Bread of Life and said: "Unless you eat my flesh and drink my blood you cannot live or follow me. You cannot be my disciples." Since he no longer needs to carry his own cross to the Mount of Calvary today, he makes his way of the cross through you and me. He lives in the youth of the world and so repeats his story of suffering.

The hungry little boy who eats his piece of bread crumb by crumb because he fears that the bread might be finished too soon and he will have to go hungry again—that is the First Station of the Cross.

Am I right? We often look and see nothing. We all must carry the cross and follow Christ to Calvary if we want to rise with him. Therefore, I believe that Christ before his death gave us his flesh and his blood so we could live and have enough courage to carry our cross and follow him step for step.

In our Stations of the Cross, we see that the poor and the hungry fall as Christ fell. Are we there to help him? Are we there with our sacrifices, with our real bread? There are thousands who would die for a taste of love, for a small taste of accomplishment. That is one of the Stations of the Cross where Jesus falls because of hunger.

And we know the Fourth Station of the Cross, where Jesus meets his mother. She becomes a mother to the suffering, a mother full of love and understanding. Are we there to understand our young people when they fall? When they feel lonely or unwanted? Are we there?

Simon of Cyrene took up the cross and followed Jesus, helped him to carry his cross. What you have done for youth during this year as a sign of love—the thousand and million things that you did for Christ in his poor—you were Simon of Cyrene in each of your acts.

And Veronica—are we like her? To the poor, the neglected, the unwanted? Are we there to wipe away their worries? To share their suffering? Or are we like the proud people who pass by and cannot see?

Jesus falls again. Have we taken care of people who lived in the streets like animals, but then died like angels? Are we there to raise them up? In your country you also find people sitting around in the parks, very lonesome, unwanted, uncared for. We brush them aside, saying, "Alcoholics. They are not our concern." But it is Jesus who needs our help to wipe his face. Can you do that? Or do you pass them by?

Jesus falls again—for you and for me. His clothes are taken away from him. Today little ones are deprived of love even before their birth—they have to die. They have to die because they are not wanted. These little ones must remain naked because we do not want them—and Jesus accepts this awful suffering. The unborn child accepts this suffering because it has no other choice. But I do have the choice to want the child, to love, to keep my brother, my sister.

Jesus was crucified. How many disabled and mentally handicapped young people fill our hospitals! How many of them live in your own hometown! Do we visit them? Do we share the way of the cross with them? Do we even know about them? And Jesus said: "If you want to be my disciples, take up your cross and follow me." He means we should lift the cross, feed him in the hungry, clothe him in the naked, accept him into our homes, and change our homes into his.

Let us begin the way of the cross with courage and great joy because we possess Jesus in Holy Communion! We have Jesus, the Bread of Life, who gives us life and strength. His suffering is our strength, our joy, our power. Without him we can do nothing. You young people, full of love and strength, do not waste your power on useless things.

Look around and see! See your brothers and sisters not only in your own homeland! Hungry people exist everywhere and they are waiting for you. The naked, the homeless, they are all looking for you. Do not walk away from them. They are *Christ* himself.

> Let the grace of God work in you
> by accepting what he gives to you
> and giving to him
> whatever he takes from you.

> God is a loving Father,
> our Father,
> and we only need
> to turn to him.

> God lives in us
> and therefore becomes
> a wonderful power for us.

Chapter Ten

BRANCHES ON JESUS THE VINE

CONTEMPLATIVE THOUGHTS

On the wall of an orphanage in Calcutta hangs a plaque with the following lines:

> Take your time to think.
> Take your time to pray.
> Take your time to laugh.
>
> That is the source of strength.
> That is the greatest power on earth.
> That is the music of the soul.
>
> Take your time to play.
> Take your time to love
> and be loved.
> Take your time to give.

This is the secret of eternal youth.
This is the privilege given by God.
The day is too short to be egoistic.

Take time to read.
Take time to be friendly.
Take time to work.

This is the source of wisdom.
This is the road to good fortune.
This is the price of success.

Take your time
to do works of charity.
They are the key to heaven.

Mother Teresa built her efforts to become Christ-like on the foundation of her faith in the words of Christ given in Matthew 25:35–40. "For I was hungry, and you gave me to eat: I was thirsty, and you gave me to drink: I was a stranger, and you took me in: naked, and you covered me: sick, and you visited me: I was in prison, and you came to me....Amen, I say to you, as long as you did it to one of these my least brethren, you did it to me" (Douay Rheims).

Mother Teresa continued to build on this thought:

When I was hungry, you gave me to eat,
When I was thirsty, you gave me to drink.
Whatever you do to the least of my brothers, you do it
    to me.

Now enter into the home of my Father.
When I was without shelter, you opened your doors.
When I was naked, you gave me your coat.
When I was tired, you helped me find rest.
When I was fearful, you took away all my fear.
When I was little, you taught me to read.
When I was lonely, you gave me your love.
When I was imprisoned, you came to my cell.
When I was sick, you cared for me.
When I was in a strange country, you gave me a home.
When I was jobless, you found me some work.
When I was wounded in battle, you bound up my
    wounds.
When I needed kindness, you held my hands.
When I was Black or Chinese or White,
scoffed at and insulted, you carried my cross.
When I was old, you gave me your smile.
When I was restless, you listened patiently.
You saw me covered with spittle and blood.
You recognized me even though I was dirty with sweat.
When I was laughed at, you stood by my side.
When I was happy, you shared my joy.

We should all become true
and fruit-bearing branches
on Jesus the vine
by accepting him into our lives
in whatever form

he chooses to come to us:
as truth—to announce it,
as life—to live it,
as light—to kindle it,
as love—to love,
as way—to follow it,
as joy—to give it,
as peace—to spread it,
as sacrifice—to bring it
into our families
and among our neighbors.

The honorable helpers, men and women, who support the sisters so that they can do their work, who are only required to be able to give of their time and love, are welcomed with the words written on a bulletin board in the motherhouse:

You come to serve Christ
in the disabled,
the sick,
and the dying.
We are happy and grateful
that you are taking the opportunity
to be witnesses of God's active love.
Think about it!
It is Christ who works through us.
We are only the tools for his work.
It is not important

how much we do,
but that what we do is done
with love.

Words on a bulletin board on the wall of Shishu Bhavan, a children's home in Calcutta:

> The people are unreasonable,
> illogical, and selfish.
> Love them anyway.
>
> When you do good,
> some will accuse you of selfish
> or ulterior motives.
> Do the good anyway.
>
> When you are successful,
> you will win false friends
> or true enemies.
> Do the successful things anyway.
>
> Honesty and openness
> make you vulnerable.
> Be honest and open anyway.
>
> What you have built up
> through years-long work
> may be destroyed overnight.
> Build it anyway.

Your help is really needed,
but the people might attack you
even while you are helping.
Help anyway.

If you are giving your best to the world
and they knock out your teeth,
give your best to the world
anyway.

We depend completely on Divine Providence.
I could give you thousands of examples
for a day and a night
of God's sensitive kindness and care.
I would like to share with you the joy
coming from our complete dependence
on Divine Providence.
I could give you example after example of
how wonderfully God has helped.
God is so good!
His protective hands rests on us.

We need the quiet
to hear God within us,
to hear him speak in our hearts.
God is a friend of stillness.

The fruit of quiet is prayer.
The fruit of prayer is faith.
The fruit of faith is love.
The fruit of love is service.
The fruit of service is peace.

About the Editor

Roswitha Kornprobst was born in 1957, is married, and has two children. She studied Catholic theology, religious pedagogy, and biology. At present she works as a teacher. She has published various articles about Mother Teresa.

Mother Teresa
Walking with Her Saints
EDITED BY HIROSHI KATAYANAGI, SJ

Focusing on different saints, this book features a quote from Mother Teresa, a scripture passage, and a photo that enhances them both.

978-0-8091-0576-2 Hardcover

My Dear Children
Mother Teresa's Last Message
MOTHER TERESA; EDITED BY HIROSHI KATAYANAGI, SJ

Compelling, candid photos of Mother Teresa, accompanied by brief passages from letters to her co-workers and speeches. A wonderful gift book.
"The photographs are worth the price of the book....A close up of her gnarled, broken-sandled feet is so 'Jesus-like' it seems sacred."

—*Connecticut Post*

0-8091-0553-5 Hardcover

Mother Teresa
A Life of Love
ELAINE MURRAY STONE

A warm and comprehensive look at the life of this most famous and recognizable figure of our century.
Ages 10 and up.

"Elaine Murray Stone has the rare ability of bringing our saints and heroes to life. It is good to see her 'Mother Teresa' living vividly in her pages....But Elaine Stone writes not about a dead saint, but a vibrantly living one, and in a style suited for both student and teacher. This is a beautifully crafted biography, and a needed one. It will be around for a long time."

—Madeleine L'Engle, Newberry Award Winner, author of 60 books, including *A Wrinkle in Time*

0-8091-6651-8 Paperback

Becoming Who You Are
Insights on the True Self from Thomas Merton and Other Saints
JAMES MARTIN, SJ

By meditating on personal examples from the author's life, as well as reflecting on the inspirational life and writings of Thomas Merton, stories from the Gospels, and the lives of other holy men and women (among them, Henri Nouwen, Therese of Lisieux and Pope John XXIII), the reader will see how becoming who you are, and becoming the person that God created, is a simple path to happiness, peace of mind and even sanctity.

1-58768-036-X Paperback

The Catholic Prayer Bible (NRSV):
Lectio Divina Edition
PAULIST PRESS

An ideal Bible for anyone who desires to reflect on the individual stories and chapters of just one, or even all, of the biblical books, while being led to prayer though meditation on that biblical passage.

978-0-8091-0587-8 Hardcover
978-0-8091-4663-5 Paperback

www.ingramcontent.com/pod-product-compliance
Lightning Source LLC
Chambersburg PA
CBHW061250040426
42444CB00010B/2325